Dedicated to my wife, Amy, and two boys, for the happiness you give me every day.
I love you and wish you happiness, forever and ever.

Stay in touch at www.piccopuppy.com and @PiccoPuppy on Instagram and Facebook.

Picco Puppy books are available in personalized, bilingual, French, Spanish, Italian, German, Chinese, and Japanese editions. Visit www.piccopuppy.com for more information.

A special thanks to my wonderful team: Ann Baratashvili (illustrator) and David Miles (designer).

Font Credits
Lost Brush by Stripes Studio
Marck Script by Denis Masharov
Cormorant Upright by Christian Thalmann
Century Schoolbook by Morris Fuller Benton
Copse by Dan Rhatigan
Josefin Sans by Santiago Orozco

First published in 2020 by Picco Puppy

Marketing Munch Pty Limited DBA Picco Puppy, PO Box 103, Killara, NSW 2071, Australia
Picco Puppy® is a registered trademark of Marketing Munch Pty Limited

ISBN 978-1-925973-19-8

I Wish You Happiness

MICHAEL WONG • ANN BARATASHVILI

Noah, I wish you
dreams and *aspirations*,
to spread your wings and
reach for the stars.

I wish you *courage* and *strength*, for the magic begins at the end of your comfort zone.

I wish you *imagination* and *creativity*, for the world is a blank canvas to paint your masterpiece.

Noah, I wish you
adventure and *curiosity*,
to go where there is no path
and leave a trail.

I wish you *health* and *well-being*, *Noah*, for they are worth more than all the riches in the world.

I wish you *peace* and *tranquility*, to
listen to the birds and gaze at the stars.

I wish you *knowledge* and *wisdom*, for they are the foundations of a successful life.

I wish you *grit* and
resilience, to never
ever give up, *Noah*.

I wish you *success*
and *prosperity*, to
trust yourself and your
ability to succeed.

Noah, I wish you
luck and *opportunity*,
for the more you try,
the luckier you get.

I wish you *faith* and *hope*, to believe everything will be all right.

Noah, I wish you *family* and *friendships*, for they are life's greatest sources of happiness.

I wish you *joy* and *laughter*, *Noah*, to laugh long and loud until you gasp for breath.

Noah, I wish you *kindness* and *generosity*, for no act of kindness is ever wasted, no matter how small.

I wish you *love* and *affection*, to fill your beautiful heart with an ocean of joy.

Noah, I wish you all those wonderful things, but most of all . . .

I wish you happiness!

Can You Spot the Famous People?

Noah, no matter what obstacles you face, believe in yourself and all that you are—
just like these famous people did. Can you spot all five in the book?

Can you spot a young Neil Armstrong?
Neil is a famous astronaut who became the first person to walk on the moon in 1969. Before that, he was an experimental research test pilot, which is a very dangerous job.

Can you spot a young Katherine Johnson?
Katherine is a mathematician whose calculations helped send the Apollo 11 rocket carrying Neil Armstrong and his fellow astronauts to the moon.

Noah, can you spot a young Amelia Earhart?
Amelia was the first female aviator to fly solo across the Atlantic Ocean. She helped to create The Ninety-Nines, an international organization of women pilots.

Can you spot a young J. K. Rowling?
Twelve publishers rejected Joanne's first book. She had to wait a year before her book was finally published. Her Harry Potter books went on to become the best-selling book series in history.

Can you spot a young Alexander Selkirk?
Alexander famously spent four years as a castaway on an uninhabited island. His survival story inspired Daniel Defoe's Robinson Crusoe, often credited as the first English novel, published in 1719.

Can You Spot the Dogs?

There are seventeen dogs and one cat in the book. Noah, can you spot them all?

Beagle	Cavalier King Charles Spaniel	Dalmatian	French Bulldog	German Shepherd	Golden Retriever
Jack Russell Terrier	Labrador Retriever	Maltese	Pomeranian	Poodle	Pug
Saint Bernard	Shiba Inu	Siamese Cat	Welsh Corgi	West Highland Terrier	Yorkshire Terrier

Hi, it's Michael here. If you enjoyed this book,
please leave a review on Amazon.
Did you know there are more books in
"The Unconditional Love Series"?
I hope you collect them all.

As an appreciation for your kind support,
claim your gift at www.piccopuppy.com/gift.

Michael Wong is an award-winning children's author. He is passionate about creating beautiful, empowering, diverse, and inclusive books for children. Michael lives with his wife and two children in Sydney, Australia.

Ann Baratashvili is an illustrator and concept artist. She won first prize in the 2009 DeviantArt/Wacom "Bring Your Vision to Life: Dreams" contest. Ann lives with her husband and son in Tbilisi, Georgia.

The Unconditional Love Series

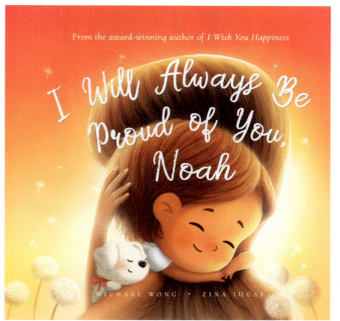

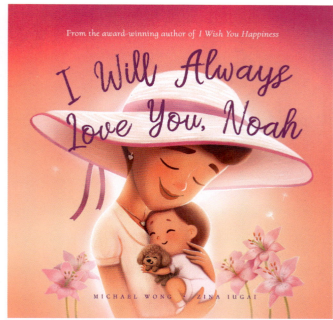

Available at Amazon and PiccoPuppy.com.

Printed in Great Britain
by Amazon